MW01030021

MANAGEMENT

BRIAN TRACY

AMACOM AMERICAN MANAGEMENT ASSOCIATION
New York • Atlanta • Brussels • Chicago • Mexico City
San Francisco • Shanghai • Tokyo • Toronto • Washington, D.C.

Bulk discounts available. For details visit:
www.amacombooks.org/go/specialsales
Or contact special sales:
Phone: 800-250-5308 / E-mail: specialsls@amanet.org
View all the AMACOM titles at: www.amacombooks.org

Library of Congress Cataloging-in-Publication Data

Tracy, Brian.
  Management / Brian Tracy.
    pages cm
  Includes index.
  ISBN-13: 978-0-8144-3419-2
  ISBN-10: 0-8144-3419-3
  1. Management. I. Title.
  HD31.T67195 2014
  658—dc23

                                                                    2013051231

About AMA

American Management Association (www.amanet.org) is a world leader in talent development, advancing the skills of individuals to drive business success. Our mission is to support the goals of individuals and organizations through a complete range of products and services, including classroom and virtual seminars, webcasts, webinars, podcasts, conferences, corporate and government solutions, business books, and research. AMA's approach to improving performance combines experiential learning—learning through doing—with opportunities for ongoing professional growth at every step of one's career journey.

Printing number
10 9 8 7 6 5 4 3 2 1

CONTENTS

Introduction

TWO HUNDRED years ago, during the early years of the Industrial Revolution, most of the world was poor. Most of the world is still poor today. Over the last 200 years, we've gone through a technological revolution, beginning with the advent of the steam engine and electricity, right up to the amazing technologies that we know and use today. It is said that high technology has vastly reduced poverty in most of the Western world and created more wealth for more people than was ever dreamed possible in all of human history.

But the fact is that it is not technology. It has not been a technological revolution but rather a *managerial* revolution. It is the managers of enterprises and organizations at all levels who have been responsible for the great bursts in progress. Technology has always followed managerial development.

In this book, I'm going to talk to you about twenty-one key ideas you can use to become a more effective manager. Why is this subject important? In my studies over the years, I've read hundreds of books, taken a business degree, and worked as a consultant, trainer, and adviser for more than 1,000 large corporations. I work every year with hundreds and sometimes thousands of managers. I have seen good managers and poor managers, and I've found that 20 percent of managers, as you can expect, get 80 percent of the results. This means that 80 percent of managers are getting only 20 percent of the results.

My aim in this book is to give you the techniques and tools, methods and ideas, for moving yourself up into the top 20 percent. And if you are in the top 20 percent already (and the fact that you are reading this book indicates that you are), you will learn how to move into the top 5 percent of managers, and then the top one percent.

The Inexact Science

Management is an inexact science. I have started, built, managed, or turned around more than thirty businesses, and I can assure you that there are no fixed answers. There are no answers that are correct all the time. The key to managerial success is learning and practice, over and over, although you probably will never get it exactly right.

When Vince Lombardi took over the Green Bay Packers, he was asked, "How are you going to change the way this team operates? Are you going to bring in new plays and ideas on how to run the ball?"

He said, "No, we're going to simply become brilliant on the basics."

In my estimation, 80 percent of managerial success is determined by practicing the basics over and over. They represent about 20 percent of management activities. In this book, you will learn, or be reminded of, the 20 percent of managerial skills that make all the difference.

If you practice the same methods that other successful managers practice, you will find that you can sometimes accomplish more in your managerial position in a few days than you've been able to accomplish in weeks or months in the past.

The Definition of a Manager

Let's start off with our definition of a manager. A manager is someone who gets results by working with and through others. A manager is someone who does the right things right.

What is an excellent manager? An excellent manager is someone who achieves superior results by consistently getting the best out of himself or herself, while releasing the potential of others so that they can make an even greater contribution to the organization.

The strength of any organization is determined by the quality of its managers at all levels. They are the "officer corps" of the business army. What they do and how well they do it are the key determinants of corporate success.

The most conservative studies estimate that the average person works at less than 50 percent of capacity, and sometimes at just 40 percent or 30 percent. A good manager creates an environment where the average person functions at 60 percent, 70 percent, 80 percent, 90 percent, and occasionally close to 100 percent of capacity, and makes a massive rather than an average contribution to the organization.

Here now are the twenty-one key ideas for becoming an excellent manager.

ONE

The Key Questions for Managerial Effectiveness

THE STARTING point for achieving greater effectiveness is asking and answering the right questions, over and over. Answering these questions will help you keep your eye on the ball. Excellent managers are highly aware of the answers to the important questions.

The key questions for managerial effectiveness are:

- *Why are you on the payroll?* Good managers are extremely results-oriented, instead of being process- or activity-oriented. They are always focused on the results they have been hired to produce. What have you been hired to accomplish?

- *What is the unique contribution that you can make?* What can you and only you contribute to your organization that, if done well, will make a significant difference?

- *What are you trying to do and how are you trying to do it?* Analyze your work and ask why you are doing something and not doing something else. Most people spend 80 percent of their time on the 80 percent of their work that only contributes 20 percent of the value of what they do. Top-performing managers always concentrate on the few things that, if done especially well, will make a real difference.

- *What are your assumptions?* Your assumptions must be questioned. What if your assumptions were wrong? What would you do then?

- *Could there be a better way?* Whatever you are doing today, there are probably many better ways to achieve the same goals. Keep your mind open.

Continually asking these questions deepens your perception, expands your range of understanding, and brings you answers, ideas, and insights that help you to be more effective—and make a more valuable contribution to your organization in a shorter period of time.

TWO

Focus on Key Result Areas

YOUR KEY result areas are your most significant areas of contribution. In the field of managerial performance, the focus on key result areas is the key to your effectiveness, your future, and success in your career.

There are seven key results areas for managers. Each is important, and, whatever your position, one of them is probably more important than any other at a given time. With changing circumstances, one key result area will rise to prominence and one will decline in importance. But you must be cognizant of what they are if you want to improve and perform at your best in each area.

Customers Count

The first key result area in a business is customer needs. The customer can be defined as "someone who depends on you, and someone you depend on for your success in your career."

It turns out that every manager has three "customers" to serve in order to be successful. The first customer is, of course, your boss. Managers must give their bosses what they want and in the form that they demand it. As long as you please your boss, your job will be secure and your future will be assured.

The second customer that you have to satisfy is the external customer. This is the customer who uses what you produce. It could be an outside customer in the marketplace, or it could be another department within the organization. This customer must be satisfied for you to be deemed to be doing an excellent job.

The third customer is your staff. Keeping them happy and focused on the most valuable uses of their time is absolutely essential for you to get the most out of each staff member.

Profit and Loss

The second key result area in business is economics. All organizational success is determined by economics. Managers are continually striving to either increase revenues or to decrease costs. As a manager, you think continually about the cost of inputs relative to the value of outputs.

Economics always refers to "maximization." You are always trying to get the highest possible return on the amount of money, time, energy, and emotion invested in a particular course of endeavor.

Focus on Quality

The third key result area of management is quality. The quality of your work largely determines your future in business.

As an executive, you set the standards for your area of responsibility, so the standards of quality that you set for your products and services, as well as for the work that you do, are especially important. For this reason, you must emphasize quality, discuss quality, and continually encourage others to think about how you could improve the quality of what you do for your internal and external customers.

Produce More with Less

The fourth key result area in business is productivity. The most successful companies use their resources efficiently and well. They achieve a higher level of output per unit of input than their competitors. They are continually seeking ways to do things better, faster, or cheaper.

A focus on increasing productivity requires clear goals, plans, checklists of essential activities, and a never-ending focus on getting more and more important things done in less time.

Innovation and Creativity

The fifth key result area in business is innovation—developing new products, services, and ways of doing business to satisfy the ever-increasing demands of your customers in a competitive market.

Innovation requires that you create a culture that encourages people to generate new ideas. These new ideas include better ways of getting things done, new approaches to the business, new products, new services, and new methods and processes for operating your business. A top executive wrote, "Our only sustainable competitive advantage is our ability to learn and apply new ideas faster than our competitors."

One of the best examples of the power of innovation is the ongoing smartphone battle between Apple and Samsung. When Apple released its iPhone in 2007, it quickly revolutionized the entire world of mobile phones. Within a year, Apple had sold tens of millions of units of its new product, with gross margins of almost 50 percent profit per unit.

At this point, Samsung, a manufacturer of consumer electronics and laptop computers, decided that the smartphone market was an excellent area for innovation and expansion. While Apple began introducing one new version of its iPhone every twelve to eighteen months, Samsung began offering three to five versions of new smartphones each year.

Within five years, the Apple iPhone went from a 50 percent market share to a market share of 12.9 percent in 2013. Samsung, because of its furious rate of innovation and new product offerings, moved from the "new kid on the block" to holding 69 percent of the world market for smartphones by 2013.

Grow Your People

The sixth key result area in business is people growth. How much time and money do you invest in training and developing the people upon which your business is dependent?

According to the American Society for Training and Development, the top 20 percent of companies, in terms of growth and profits, invest 3 percent or more of their gross revenue back into training the people that they depend on to generate those revenues in the first place.

According to an article in *Human Resource Executive* magazine, the payoff in people training is extraordinarily high, ranging from $10 back to the bottom line to as much as $32 back for every dollar spent in training people to become even better at what they do.

Organizational Development

The seventh key result area in business is organizational development, which entails thinking about and doing the things that create a positive and harmonious organizational climate. These are the aspects of your business that make people feel happy to work there and fully engaged, enabling them to produce at their very best.

You should continually be asking yourself what you could do to improve in each of the seven key result areas: customer needs, economics, quality, productivity, innovation, employee growth and training, and organizational development. What are the 20 percent of activities that account for 80 percent of your results? What are the 20 percent of problems that account for 80 percent of your stress or underachievement? What are the 20 percent of things you can do that can enable you to take advantage of 80 percent of your opportunities in your field?

Excellent managers have clarity. They continually focus their efforts on key result areas of their businesses.

THREE

Set Standards of Performance

ONCE YOU have determined your key result areas, the next step is to set standards of performance for each one. As Yogi Berra said, "You can't hit a target that you can't see."

For you to perform at your best as a manager, you must set standards of performance, and even standards of *excellent performance* for each job and for each function in your area of responsibility. People need to know exactly what you expect and to what level of quality.

These standards need to be specific, measurable, and time-bounded. Remember, "What gets measured gets done."

When you ask other people to do a job, you must also tell them your desired schedule of completion and how, exactly, you are going to measure whether that job has been done properly.

Perhaps the greatest leap forward in business in recent years is the concept of "measurement-based management." This is where you assign specific numbers, benchmarks, and standards to every area of activity in your company, right down to how many times the phone will ring before it is answered.

The Hawthorne Effect

There is a principle in psychology called the Hawthorne effect, which comes from the pioneering work on labor productivity conducted at the Western Electric Hawthorne Works in 1928. What they found was that when people are clear about a particular number or target, they continually compare themselves against that number and both consciously and unconsciously improve their performance in that area. This process of continuous improvement starts with you and your employees being clear about the number in the first place.

The achievement of standards of performance must be the only basis for rewards in an organization. Rewards in a top company go to performance, excellence, increased sales, and measurable achievement. Rewards must be based on performance and results alone.

In his wonderful book *The Greatest Management Principle in the World*, Michael LeBoeuf says, "What gets rewarded gets done." The key question you have to ask yourself continually in your work is, "What is getting rewarded?"

Are you rewarding the performance you desire or require? Whenever you see an organization or a department that is performing below standard, you will almost always find that the wrong things are being rewarded.

Perverse Incentives

In one company I worked for, the telemarketers received a reward or a bonus for each potential customer that they could talk into attending a live sales presentation of the company's services. This system ensured that several hundred people would come to a large presentation each month. However, the number of those potential customers who actually bought the company's services was quite low. The managers discovered that they were rewarding the wrong things.

They then changed their compensation system to a base salary plus a commission on the sales made to the people who were invited to the presentation. The telemarketers, responding to the new incentive, became much more careful about inviting only qualified prospects who could become immediate customers. The company's business doubled and then doubled again within the next few months.

Inspect What You Expect

Once you have set performance standards, you must inspect what you expect. When you assign a task and set a standard of performance, also arrange to check back with the employee regularly, to be sure that the job is being done on schedule and to the previously agreed-to standard.

Employees value the importance of their work much more when they know that the boss cares enough to set standards and then check with them to make sure that the standards are being met. The reverse of this regular inspection is when the boss assigns a job and then turns to other things, leaving employees alone to perform without measurement or feedback.

Delegation is not abdication. Even though you have assigned a job to another person, you are still responsible for its successful completion. When you inspect what you expect, only then will people believe that you consider the job important enough for them to strive to meet the standards that you have mutually set.

Clarity Is Essential

In business and in life, *clarity* is one of the most important words associated with success. Thousands of employees have been surveyed and asked about the characteristics of the best bosses they have ever had. They universally agree on this point: "I always knew what my boss expected me to do."

The reason you must be clear about key result areas and standards of performance is that, without them, neither you nor your employees can perform at high levels. If you cannot perform the job in an excellent fashion, you cannot earn recognition and promotion. You cannot perform with distinction. As a manager, the people under you cannot do their very best unless they know exactly what that is and how it will be measured.

The kindest thing you can do for your staff members is to help them to be absolutely clear about what it is you need them to do and to what standard of performance. When people are clear about the target they are aiming at, they will often amaze you with the quality and quantity of their production and output.

FOUR

Concentrate Your Powers

WARREN BUFFETT, Bill Gates Jr., and Bill Gates Sr. were chatting together at a social event when an executive approached them with a question. "What would you gentlemen say is the most important quality for success in business?"

According to bystanders, all three of these highly successful businessmen turned to the questioner and said simultaneously: "Focus!"

In a world of nonstop distraction, from telephone calls and voice mail to text messages, the Internet, and the people all around you, your ability to focus single-mindedly is absolutely essential for your success. In fact, all real success in life comes from developing the ability to concentrate your time, attention, and talents on those few tasks that can make all the difference to your success in your work. This is the real purpose for defining key result areas and setting standards of performance.

All of time management boils down to asking and answering a single question: "What is the most valuable use of my time right now?" Perhaps the best definition of time management is that it is "your ability to choose the sequence of events." Your ability to organize your time in sequence so that you are clear about what you do first, what you do second, and what you do not do at all, is the key to doubling and tripling your productivity and the productivity of the people who report to you.

The Law of Three

Through more than thirty years of studying and teaching time management, I have discovered a powerful principle that is potentially life- and career-transforming. This Law of Three says that no matter how many tasks you perform in the course of a month, there are only three tasks and activities that account for 90 percent of the value of the contribution you make to your business.

In this sense, the word *contribution* is quite powerful in determining your success in your career. The more valuable your contribution to the achievement of the overall goals of your business, the more valuable and important you become as well.

Three Magic Questions

How do you determine your "big three"? Simple. You ask the three magic questions.

1. *If I could only do one thing, all day long, what one task or activity would contribute the most value to my business?* Make a list of everything you do in the course of a month, and then you review this list. The one activity that you engage in that contributes the most will probably jump out at you. Put a circle around that one task.

2. *If I could only do two things, all day long, which would be the second activity that would contribute the greatest value to my business?* Usually, this item will jump out at you as well. You may have to compare and contrast different things you do to be sure that you have the right answer, but it is usually not difficult.

3. *If I could only do three things, all day long, what would be the third task that would contribute the most value to my business?* I have conducted this exercise with many thousands of executives and business owners. Without exception, in every case, in a matter of a minute or two, people become crystal clear about the three most important things that they can do (or should be doing) that would contribute the greatest value to themselves and their businesses.

This Law of Three means that everything other than those three big jobs falls into the 10 percent category. Every other activity is of low value or no value. The primary reason for failure in the executive suite is that too many people spend too much time working on too many tasks that have little or no value to themselves or their business. They make no contribution at all.

Define the Big Three for Others

Once you have developed absolute clarity about the most valuable use of your time, you should help each person who reports to you to identify his or her "big three" as well. You can transform the productivity and performance of your entire work unit by helping your employees to develop absolute clarity and focus on the three tasks that they can do, all day long, that will make the greatest contribution.

One of the greatest kindnesses that you can do for your staff members is to encourage them to answer this question for themselves. It is only when employees know their most important tasks that they can perform to distinction. It is only when they are working on their key tasks, and doing them well, in a timely fashion, that they can make their maximum contribution and can both be paid more and promoted faster.

The three words for maximum performance are *clarity*, *focus*, and *concentration*. Once you have decided on the most important task you can complete, your next duty to yourself is to concentrate single-mindedly on that one task until it is 100 percent complete.

Task completion is the key to success in work and in life. Important task completion is even more central to success. And completing your most important tasks before anything else will do more to put your career onto the fast track than any other activity you can engage in at work. (Please read my AMACOM minibook on *Time Management* for more ideas for increasing your productivity, performance, and output.)

FIVE

The Vital Functions of Management

THERE ARE several vital functions of management that determine the success or failure of the executive. The "vital functions concept" comes from medicine and physical health. It is an original and helpful way for you to look at your activities in your career.

Suppose you went to a doctor for a complete physical checkup. The doctor tells you that you have a series of potential medical problems. You are overweight and have high blood pressure; you are not physically fit and are eating the wrong foods and engaging in poor health habits.

If you want to be genuinely healthy, you are going to have to make modifications and changes in each of these vital function areas. The vital functions themselves are your heart rate, temperature, blood pressure, brain wave activity, respiration rate, and other physiological measures. Each is a clinical definition of life or death. If you are lacking any one of these vital signs, you are clinically dead.

Armed with information, you decide to make a series of changes in your health habits. To begin with, you decide to go for a walk for thirty minutes a day, or approximately 210 minutes a week, which is the ideal number of minutes for you to eventually enjoy excellent physical health. But when you start walking thirty minutes a day to reduce your weight, what happens to your heart rate, your blood pressure, and even your brain wave activity?

The answer is that as you improve in one area, you simultaneously begin to improve in every other as well.

It is the same in management. As you improve in each of the important functions of management, this improvement spills over and brings about an improvement in other areas as well. By focusing and concentrating on improving one particular management skill, you simultaneously begin to improve across the board in all your management skills.

You actually create a multiplier effect that can lead to rapid overall improvement in your skill level and in the value of the contribution you make to your company.

Seven Vital Functions of Management

In management, you must perform at an adequate level in each of seven areas if you want to be able to do your job in an excellent fashion. The absence of any one of these seven vital functions of management can lead to your failure as an executive.

MAKE PLANS

Planning is a key management skill and the first vital function. Your ability to plan carefully everything that you want or need to get done, in advance, allows you to accomplish vastly more than a person who is working without a plan.

The rule for success in management is to "think on paper." Write down your objectives and become absolutely clear about the goals you wish to achieve. Make detailed lists of every step that you will have to take to achieve those goals. Make checklists of those activities in chronological order to create a recipe or a blueprint that you can follow, step by step.

The greater clarity that people have about goals and plans, the faster they can get to work and the better they can do their jobs.

GET ORGANIZED

The second vital function of management is organizing. Once you have done the planning, you need to bring together the people, money, resources, and facilities necessary to turn the plan into a reality.

The very best executives are excellent at planning and organizing. As a result, they can bring together and coordinate the activities of large numbers of people to achieve extraordinarily complex tasks.

At both the Los Angeles Summer Olympics in 1984 and the Salt Lake City Winter Olympics in 2002, the Olympic Committee had descended into confusion, and huge financial losses were expected by both cities. Then, Los Angeles hired baseball commissioner Peter Ueberroth, and Salt Lake

City brought in Mitt Romney, the 2012 Republican candidate for president.

In both cases, these extremely talented executives immediately went to work planning, organizing, and coordinating tens of thousands of people over vast geographical areas, dealing with thousands of details, and each man pulled the games out of the financial fires. Because of the planning and organizing skills of these two men, the games went from huge projected losses to high levels of profitability and enormous success from the point of view of the participants and spectators.

Again, the key to organizing well is to "think on paper." Discuss what has to be done with everyone who will be essential to carrying out the plan. The more time you spend planning and organizing before you take action, the more likely it is that you will be successful.

FIND THE BEST PEOPLE

The third vital function of management is staffing or recruiting. Your ability to select the right people to help you to achieve the goals you have set is central to your success as a manager. In many cases, one weak or incompetent person in a key job can lead to the failure of the enterprise. The financial press frequently has stories about senior executives who have made bad decisions and almost bankrupted huge companies.

To make your most valuable contribution, you must interview and hire the best people for the job. Simultaneously, you must dehire people who are not capable of doing excellent work in the achievement of your goals.

LEARN TO DELEGATE

The fourth vital function is delegating. Delegation is an essential skill that you want to learn because it enables you to maximize the productivity and elicit the very best contribution from the people who report to you.

KEEP ON TOP OF THE WORK

The fifth vital function in management is supervising. Supervision requires that people be absolutely clear about what it is that you want them to do, and to what standard of performance. You then regularly check with them to make sure that the job is being done on time and to the standards that you have agreed upon.

When people know that you care about the work enough to check its progress on a regular basis, they are far more likely to do excellent work and to do it on schedule.

KEEP PEOPLE INFORMED

The sixth vital function of management is reporting. When you do a good job, or even when you have problems and difficulties, it is essential that people around you know what is going on, either good or bad.

Be sure that communications between you and your boss are clear and consistent. Establish a regular routine of one-on-one, face-to-face meetings to keep your boss fully informed about what you are doing and how it is going.

It is also essential that you communicate with your peers and colleagues, those people over whom you have no control but who need to know what you are doing in order to do their jobs to an acceptable high standard.

Finally, practice open-door management with your staff. Tell your staff everything that is going on: the good, the bad, and the ugly. According to "Great Place to Work" interviews and studies conducted annually, happy employees working for an organization say that they always feel "in the know" about the things that affect their work and their company.

SET CLEAR STANDARDS

The seventh vital function of management is measuring. As mentioned previously, this is where you set clear standards for what you want done so that all employees know exactly how to measure their performance.

You have heard the saying, "If you can't measure it, you can't manage it." Force yourself and your staff to put a number on every activity. The good news is that all business activities can be measured, usually with financial numbers. If not financial numbers, they can be measured with some other number. Your job is to help people select the correct number to measure the performance of a job in a particular area, and then to focus on meeting or exceeding that number.

So, commit today to improvement in the vital functions of management—planning, organizing, hiring, delegating, supervising, reporting, and measuring—and then dedicate yourself to continuous and never-ending improvement in each area.

SIX

Management by Objectives

USED WITH the right people in the right situation, management by objectives is a vital tool that can dramatically increase your output and build your subordinates. Most managers don't use MBO, or if they do, they use it incorrectly or inappropriately.

MBO is used for competent employees who have demonstrated their ability to get the job done to an acceptable level of quality. When you have a job that needs to be done, you bring in a person you feel is capable of doing this job in an excellent fashion. It could be the achievement of a certain level of sales, the start and completion of a project, or the transformation of an entire department or division. Your goal is to assign the complete task to one person who has demonstrated an ability to do this type of job in the past.

Remember, successful task completion is the key to getting onto the fast track in business. The ability to plan, organize, and complete a task or a project to an acceptable level of performance is the most important skill that you can develop in your business life.

Clarity Is Your Friend

With MBO, clarity is your best friend. Once you have selected the person to whom you are going to give the job, you mutually agree with that person on what exactly it is that needs to be accomplished and how it will be measured. It takes a good deal of discussion, back and forth, until you are both clear on a definition of the task to be completed and in agreement about how it will be measured.

Some years ago, my boss asked me to take over a real estate development project on the edge of a small town about 300 miles from the home office. I was hungry and ambitious and accepted the assignment immediately.

The next day, I flew to the nearest large city and then drove to the town and inspected the property that my company had purchased. It was of no value until it was developed into parcels and sold. That was my job, even though I had never done it before.

My boss, a brilliant businessman, had purchased this property off a plot map from a real estate agent. He had never visited the town or seen the property when he turned it over to me to turn into a viable financial investment.

I was an eager student. I asked questions of everyone, took notes, then compared the notes. I hired expert engineers who gave me good advice and introduced me to other experts in other areas of activity. As a result, within eighteen months, I was able to complete a development plan for the property. It was subdivided, with lots and streets for 335 homes, an industrial park, and a commercial shopping center.

With these plans, I worked with the town council to get approval, retained an engineering firm to put in all the underground utilities and build the roads, and then sold all the parcels in the land holding to developers, who subsequently built out the residential neighborhoods, the industrial park, and the retail shopping center.

Manage with a Clear Goal

The interesting part of this story, aside from the amount that I learned and the more than $3 million in profit that I took back to my company, was that my boss never did visit the property. He entrusted 100 percent of the responsibility to me to complete all the hundreds of details necessary to bring this project to successful fruition. He was a master at the use of management by objectives.

Once you have agreed on the task to be completed, you then agree on measurements and standards of performance, as well as the schedule for work and completion. The exact details can be discussed, negotiated, and even changed later if you get new information.

Remain Available

The next part of management by objectives is for you to remain available to the person who's been assigned the task.

You make it clear that the individual is completely responsible for the task that you've assigned, but that if the person needs any help or assistance, you are always available.

Leave the person free to do the job. Once both of you have agreed on the end result or the final goal of the project, allow the individual to accomplish the goal using his own ideas, methods, and techniques. Even if you think that you would or could do it differently, give people the greatest amount of freedom possible to find creative ways to deal with the "situation on the ground" as the project evolves. Don't be reluctant to offer ideas and advice, but let the people you've assigned the work to make the final decision about how to do the job.

Finally, plan to review the project on a prearranged basis, once a week, once every two weeks, or even once a month. The more important the task that you have assigned, the more important it is that you check on it regularly to make sure that it is on schedule and on budget.

Multiply Your Input

Management by objectives is an effective way to multiply your output by passing off critical jobs and areas of responsibility to experienced staff. The assignment of complete responsibility for a project is also one of the most powerful ways of all to grow people in competence and confidence. All successful executives have become excellent at managing by objectives, because it enables them to accomplish vastly more than the average manager.

SEVEN

Management by Exception

MANAGEMENT BY exception is an excellent time saver and people builder. Here's how it works: Once you have given an assignment and you have made it clear, measurable, and time-bounded, you then tell the person, "Only come back to me if there is a variance from what we have agreed on." In using management by exception, "No news is good news." If you don't hear anything from the employee, then you can safely assume that all is well and that the job is on schedule.

You can use management by exception in other areas as well. When I am on the phone with someone who is reluctant to set an appointment at a certain time, I say, "Let's manage by exception. Let us agree to meet or talk at three o'clock on Thursday afternoon. If something comes up and this timing does not work for you, you can call me back and we can change the time to a more convenient one. But if I don't hear from you, I will assume that we will be talking/meeting at 3:00 p.m."

This practice gives maximum freedom to people, frees you from "telephone tag" and the need to be in continual communication with the other person, and signals a high level of trust in the ability of the other person do the job.

Freedom and Responsibility

Two of the best motivators in business are freedom and responsibility. People want to enjoy the maximum of freedom in performing their tasks and getting their jobs done. At the same time, making people responsible for successful completion of tasks can raise their self-esteem and self-confidence. The two go hand-in-hand.

As a manager, you can multiply and leverage your effectiveness times the number of people who can take on complete tasks and do them without your direct supervision and involvement. Always be looking for ways to hand off a task by using management by objectives or management by exception, or both of them at the same time.

The more work that can be completed by other people without your direct effort or involvement, the more you can get done. Simultaneously, you will have more time to perform those tasks that only you can do, which are the tasks that are essential to your success in your position.

EIGHT

Delegate Effectively

YOUR ABILITY to delegate well to others is a vital function of management (as covered in Chapter 5) and a critical determinant of your ability to succeed as an executive. Delegating is both an art and a science. It is an essential skill that allows you to move from what you can do to what you can control. Through delegation, you multiply your influence in your business by unlocking and using the full potential of other people.

The starting point of delegation is for you to develop absolute clarity about the job that needs to be done. Exactly what is the job? How will it be measured? When does the job need to be completed? What level of skill, ability, or competence will a person require to do this job in an exceptional fashion?

Select the Right Person

An important part of delegation is selecting the right person for the assignment of a particular task. You need to carefully match the task to the skills of the employee. Can this person do this job? Does this person have the required skills and experience to accomplish this task in an excellent fashion?

This decision is very much a matter of judgment, experience, and thoughtfulness on your part. One of the big mistakes that managers make in delegation is assigning a task to someone who does not have the skills, confidence, ability, or motivation to accomplish it.

Your choice of person, then, will largely determine the quality of the end result, and even whether the task assignment succeeds or fails.

Explain the Results You Want

When you delegate, explain the results that you want, and explain why you want those results. When you assign a task, the "why" is more important than the "how." If people know why you want it done this way, or why the task is important, they will have much greater flexibility to make decisions in the accomplishment of the task. The subordinate will be more creative and innovative in accomplishing the results that you desire.

Avoid Misunderstandings

When you give a task verbally with nothing in writing, the possibilities of misunderstandings are enormous. By the time your employees get back to their office or desk, they will have almost forgotten what you asked them to do, and when, and to what standard. Have employees write down the assignment and then read it back to you.

Once you have had a back-and-forth conversation about the job, and the employee has repeated back to you exactly what you have asked him or her to do, and you are both clear about the assignment, you then turn over 100 percent responsibility for the completion of the task to the other person.

Delegate the Whole Task

It is important that you delegate a complete job, rather than just part of a job. The job that you delegate must be the responsibility of the individual, and the completion of the task must be under that person's control entirely. Aside from yourself, the other person should not need to get the assistance or support of anyone else to do the job that you have assigned.

People thrive on responsibility for complete tasks. When you give people 100 percent of a job to do, and make them 100 percent responsible, they will be much more motivated to get the job done on schedule.

Don't Interfere or Take Back the Job

Resist the temptation to go and look over the employee's shoulder. Resist the temptation to continually offer ideas and comments on how to do the job better. Resist the temptation to interfere. When you give your employees the job, express complete confidence in their ability to get the job done as agreed.

Don't take back the job, either. If your employee asks you if you would make a phone call for him, or get him some information, or perform a certain task that he needs done in order to do the job that you have assigned him, then he has just delegated the task back to you. Now your employee does not need to do anything until you have completed your work. He can go back to his office and play on his computer until you perform the task that you have promised. Don't let this happen.

Review Progress Regularly

Finally, schedule regular meetings to review progress. It is during regular meetings that you get a chance to keep on top of things. Like a doctor taking the pulse of her patients, you take the pulse of the task by regularly asking, "How's it going?"

A major reason for scheduling regular review meetings is to get feedback on how well people are doing with their assignments and how appropriate the task is for a particular person. Sometimes you may accidentally delegate a task that is beyond a person's capability. The employee may want to do the job, but does not know exactly how to do it.

If you find that the task you have assigned is too much for your employees and they are in over their heads, you may need to restructure the task and break it up into smaller pieces. Or you may have to give an employee additional input or resources, or get someone else to perform part of the task that a person is not capable of completing alone. A particular task may require several skills. Sometimes the person you are assigning work to has several of the necessary skills but is lacking one of them. In this case, you can take this particular responsibility away from the individual and give it to someone who is more competent in that job area.

NINE

Build Peak Performers

ONE OF YOUR primary responsibilities as a manager is to build a team of peak performing individuals for your company. People who are positive, motivated, and fully engaged with their work are vastly more productive than the average staff member. They get much more done, produce work of a higher quality, and are more creative and innovative in everything they do.

High-performance organizations are those in which people feel terrific about themselves and are happy in their relationships with their superiors. People who are happy in their work, and who feel good about themselves, produce far more and better work than those who are not.

The foundation of peak performance is high self-esteem. Self-esteem is defined as "how much you like yourself." The more a person likes and respects himself, the better he performs, the better he works with other people, and the more confidence and competence he has.

Unlock the Individual's Potential

Psychologists have identified seven key managerial behaviors or conditions that you can create to motivate the people under your control, in turn raising their self-esteem and increasing their performance.

Challenge Them

The first motivator is challenge. The number one desire of people in the workplace is work that is interesting, meaningful, and draws on the very best talents they have. People want to feel challenged and fully involved in their work.

To satisfy this need, you must give people jobs that are beyond their capabilities so that they have to stretch, in terms of their time investment and effort, to get the job done well. It is only when people are stretching to improve themselves and how they do their work that they feel fully alive, and that they feel like winners.

Give Them Freedom

The second motivator is freedom (as mentioned previously in Chapter 7). People enjoy having a maximum of freedom to do their jobs. Practice giving each individual as much freedom as possible to achieve an agreed-on goal. The key to giving people this freedom revolves around your skills in using management by objectives and management by exception, and your ability to delegate well.

Give Them Respect

The third motivator in building a peak performance team is respect. People have a great need to be respected by other people whose opinions they value, especially their bosses. Employees need to be able to express their thoughts, feelings, and concerns to their boss—and they need to feel that the boss genuinely respects their ideas, whether or not the boss accepts or agrees with them. The more your employees feel that you respect them, the more they respect you and want to do a good job for you.

The Friendship Factor

The fourth motivator in the world of work is warmth. In the workplace today, one of the most important elements is what is called the "friendship factor."

People like to work for others who they think care about them as individuals. You express warmth when you ask people for their opinions or judgment. You convey warmth to your staff members when you talk to them and ask them questions about nonwork-related issues, such as sports and hobbies. You can ask them about their families, their personal lives and activities, their children, and so on. Whenever you express a genuine interest in these subjects, you convey that you care about the other person as a human being, rather than simply as an employee in your company.

Keep in Touch

The fifth motivator is control. Assigning someone a job and then forgetting about it is much more demoralizing to that person than if you give an assignment and then regularly check in with the worker. The more you check on the performance of a person in completing an assigned task, the more that person feels that the job is important—and, therefore, the person is important as well.

Perform a regular series of "nonjudgmental performance reviews." Ask questions like, "How's it going?" Ask if there is any way that you can help or if there are any resources that you can provide to help the person do the job. This gesture lets the employee know that you consider the task to be important and that you are concerned about both the task and the person performing it.

Let Them Win

The sixth motivator is to provide success experiences. Whenever you assign a job that your employees can do well, and when they complete the task, they have a success experience and feel like winners. Everything that you can do or say that causes your employees to feel like winners raises their self-esteem, improves their overall performance, and increases the value of their contribution to the organization.

Expect the Best

The seventh motivator is positive expectations. This is one of the most powerful of all tools to raise self-esteem and self-confidence in others. When you express confidence in your staff members, they will usually do everything possible to show you that you are right. Continually convey to your staff members that you believe in their ability to do an excellent job.

Some years ago, I hired a young man to run the parts department at a large automobile importation and distribution business that I was setting up. The reason I hired him was because he had the required experience with a previous company. Unfortunately, he had been fired unceremoniously from that job because of a clash with his boss. This experience had really shaken his self-confidence. As a result, he was shy and insecure. He continually downplayed his ability and tried to convince me that he had limited experience, stating as a reminder, "As you know, I was fired from my last job."

Nonetheless, like a force of erosion, I kept telling him how good he was. I just kept telling him that I believed he had the ability to be an absolutely excellent parts manager. And of all the people I hired to help me build that business, he turned out to be the best performer of all.

Make it clear that you believe in your people. Tell them that you believe in them. Even if you are not quite sure, pretend a little. Your positive expectations of other people will seldom lead to disappointment.

TEN

Achieve Managerial Leverage

ONE OF YOUR goals as a manager is to increase the quality and quantity of your output relative to your input. There are several ways that you can increase or even multiply your productivity as a manager.

First, work harder. When you arrive at work, resolve to "work all the time you work." Don't waste time. Don't chitchat with coworkers. Don't drink the coffee, surf the Internet, or read the newspaper. Instead, work all the time you work.

An unfortunate truth is that most people are lazy. It's not politically correct to say, but everyone knows it. Most people seek the path of least resistance in every action and continually strive to do the minimum of work possible over the course of the day. In fact, 50 percent of so-called "working time" is spent gabbing with coworkers, surfing the Web, reading the newspaper, taking care of personal business, going shopping, coming in later and leaving earlier, and so on. Most people are lazy and not very productive.

You can separate yourself from your coworkers by simply making a habit of "working all the time you work." Work harder, and then harder still. Develop a reputation for being the hardest-working person in your company. Nothing will put you onto the fast track with your superiors more dependably than getting a reputation for being a hard worker.

Pick Up the Pace

Two, work faster. Pick up the pace. Develop a fast tempo in your work. Move quickly, as though you have a lot to do in too little time.

Working harder and working faster are habits that you can develop with practice and repetition. Get busy. Get going. Get started and keep going. Don't waste time.

Work Longer Hours

The third way to increase your productivity is to work longer. The average person puts in thirty-two to forty hours per week, and half of that time in the workplace is usually wasted on nonwork activities. Incomes must be diluted and reduced to account for the fact that most people are not particularly productive. When they do work, they usually work on activities that are fun and easy rather than activities that are big, valuable, and important.

You can double your productivity overnight with a simple formula practiced by top people in any field: Start a little earlier, work a little harder, and stay a little later.

If normal working hours are nine to five, you should make a habit of starting at 7:30 or 8 a.m. and working until 6 p.m. Work at lunchtime as well. This simple restructuring of your day will add three hours of productive time to your activities and virtually double your productivity overnight.

Set Priorities

Do more important things. Make a list before you begin and set priorities on your list. Remember the 80/20 rule, which says that 80 percent of the value of your contribution will be contained in 20 percent of the things you do.

Even more, according to the Law of Three, 90 percent of the value of your contribution will probably be contained in only three tasks or activities. Do you know what they are? If you could only do three things all day long, what would they be? Your answers will be the answer to the question: "Why am I on the payroll?"

Hold Your Feet to the Fire

Here's a great question that you should ask and answer at the beginning of every workday. "If I could only complete one task before I was called out of town for a month, what one task would it be?"

Whatever your answer, start on that task first thing, before you do anything else. Don't check your e-mail, get another cup of coffee, or read the headlines. Don't socialize with your friends. Put your head down and throw yourself into your most important task. Then, resolve to stay at that task until it is 100 percent complete.

If you start off every day by completing one important task, your productivity will increase dramatically. Even better, you will feel terrific about yourself. You will feel like a winner, like a high performer, because you are.

Tap into Teamwork

A well-organized team consisting of a few people working together can produce far more work than a large number of people working individually. So, divide up the work among several people, and then work together in harmony.

Whenever possible, delegate, downsize, outsource, and eliminate tasks so that you can get more of the most important things done in the shortest period of time. Assign or delegate everything that anyone else can do at least 70 percent as well as you. Work in harmony with your team members to increase your overall productivity.

Batch Your Tasks

When you do several similar tasks at the same time, you quickly move to the downward slope of the learning curve. Each repeated task takes less time than the previous task. After you have done seven to ten similar tasks, like checking e-mail, dictating correspondence, writing reports, or anything that is repetitive, you will be completing each task in

20 percent of the time that it took you to complete the first task in the series.

On the other hand, starting a task and then doing something else, coming back to that task and then stopping and doing something else again, can increase the amount of time it takes you to do something by as much as 500 percent. Single-minded focus and concentration is absolutely essential to high productivity.

Think of yourself as a factory, with inputs, work processes, and outputs. Focus single-mindedly on the most important outputs of your work, and when you do start work, resolve to work all the time you work.

Hire the Right People

YOUR ABILITY to hire the right people to help you get the job done will determine your success as much as any other factor. If you cannot hire good people with the right skills, knowledge, and temperament to assist you, you will end up having to do much of the work yourself. Managers who cannot multiply themselves through other people can never be promoted to positions of higher responsibility.

In his bestselling book, *Thinking, Fast and Slow*, Daniel Kahneman explains that there are activities that require "fast thinking," quick, impulsive, instinctive, and intuitive reasoning, and about which you can make fast decisions, like changing lanes in traffic.

On the other hand, there are other activities that require "slow thinking." They require that you slow down, gather information, reflect carefully, and decide slowly. This is why Peter Drucker said, "Fast people decisions are invariably wrong people decisions."

Think on Paper

To hire the right person, begin by thinking on paper. Write out a description of the perfect person for this particular position. Put down every characteristic, quality, experience, skill, or talent that the ideal candidate would have, exactly as if you were sending an order to a factory for a custom-made product.

Next, write a description of the job (or jobs) that you want this person to do. Describe the expected results or outcomes of the job, and make them measurable. Describe the proven talents and skills that the person will need to have to achieve those results. Then describe the temperament and personality of the ideal person that you would want to hire.

Be perfectly selfish when you engage in this process. Resolve that you are only going to hire somebody that you like and respect and whose company you enjoy. "Likability" is a critical factor in all human relationships, and you should set it as one of your standards for hiring people.

The SWAN Formula

The four letters of the SWAN formula give you a recipe that you can follow for selecting the best people.

S stands for "smart." Look for smart people, intelligent people, curious people, people who seem to be positive, bright, and interested in both you and your work.

W stands for "works hard." Remember most people are lazy and just looking for a place where they can be lazy on someone else's payroll. You are looking for people who have a reputation for hard, hard work.

During the interview, there's a good way to test for how hard a person is likely to work. Say, "Occasionally, we have to work evenings and weekends to complete important jobs for our customers. How would you feel about that?"

The best candidates will immediately say, "If I get this job, I will do what it takes to be successful." If the candidate hems and haws and starts talking about needing time off for his personal or social life, that is all you need to know. If hired, this person will not be particularly productive. This person will want to continue vacation on your payroll.

The third letter, *A*, stands for "ambitious." The very best employees are those who see your job offer as a springboard to even better things for them in the future. They are convinced that accepting your job offer and doing an excellent job for you will open doors for them that will help them in their career.

The last letter in the SWAN formula stands for "nice." Always hire nice people. Always hire people that you personally enjoy. It should not be the only criterion for making a decision, but it ranks up there as very important. It turns out that nice people get along better with others, perform better as part of a team, are more cheerful when there are ups and downs in the business, and are more of a pleasure to have around than people who are negative or doubtful.

The Rule of Three

The Rule of Three is a formula that I have developed over the years. Many senior executives say that it literally revolutionizes the hiring process in their business. It also increases the likelihood that you will make the right choice in about 90 percent of hires.

The first application of the formula says that you should interview at least three candidates for any job, and perhaps more. By interviewing three candidates, you get an opportunity to contrast and compare potential hires. Never hire the first and only person that you interview. Cast a wide net and interview a variety of people for the job so that you can see what is available in the talent pool.

The second application is to interview the candidate that you like three different times. The scheduled interviews may be tomorrow or next week, or three days in a row. Go slowly. Take your time. A person who looks great in the first interview may look average in the second interview and terrible in the third interview. This happens with incredible regularity.

The third application is to interview the candidate you like in three different places. The first interview can be in your office, the second interview can be down the hall in a meeting room, and the third interview can be across the street in a coffee shop.

As you move people to different environments, they reveal different aspects of their personality that you did not see in your office. Remember that your job candidates will never look as good as they did the first time that you interview them. In the second and third interviews, or in the second and third locations, the initially appealing candidate can start to look worse and worse. So reflect carefully and decide slowly (this is what we mean by "slow thinking").

Three Other People

The fourth application of this hiring formula is to have the candidate interviewed by at least three other people. Never rely on your own judgment in selecting a person to work for your company. Always invite the involvement and opinions of other people before you make a decision.

I once interviewed an individual for a position as an executive in my company. I was quite impressed and on the verge of hiring him when I remembered my own rule. So I took him around the office and had him speak to each of the key players on my team, one at a time, so they could ask him questions and form their own judgments.

At the end of the day, they came to me as a group and told me that I absolutely must not hire this person. He was totally inappropriate for our company. He had flaws and weaknesses that I had been unable to detect, but that they had observed in their conversations with him. I dropped the consideration of the candidate immediately.

The very best executives in every industry have developed a reputation, over time, of selecting the very best people to work with and for them. This is an essential part of your becoming an excellent manager and fulfilling your potential in your industry.

The key is to go slow. There is too much at stake.

TWELVE

Fire the Incompetents

THE MOST STRESSFUL job in management is firing an employee. The second most stressful job in management is being fired yourself. But if you don't get some experience with the first job, you are going to get some experience with the second.

A manager who hires an incompetent person is himself incompetent. A manager who keeps an incompetent person in place is even more incompetent. The longer you keep the wrong person in a job, the more incompetent you look to everybody around you. You look incompetent to your superiors, your peers, and your subordinates. Keeping the wrong person in place demoralizes your staff members. They conclude that if an incompetent person gets paid the same as they do, and receives the same privileges, what's the use of trying to do a good job?

Of course, everyone knows who is competent and who is not incompetent. They know very quickly. In every office, every staff member knows the level of competence of every other person. There is nowhere to run to and nowhere to hide.

Don't Be Cruel

The cruelest thing that you can do to a person, once you have decided in your heart that this person is not going to work out in your business, is to keep the person in the job. The kindest thing that you can do for incompetent workers is to set them free. Let them go so that they can find a job in which they have a future and where there are more possibilities.

Why is it that many managers sacrifice their own careers, and often their own mental health, by avoiding the hard work of firing an incompetent person? The answer is often self-delusion. The manager thinks that he is doing the incompetent person a favor by keeping him on the payroll. Sometimes the manager even thinks that the incompetent person is suddenly going to change, do a complete reversal, and become a competent member of the staff.

The real reason that the manager does not fire is cowardice. The manager is not being kind and compassionate. The manager is being cruel and heartless. The manager is inflicting damage on the other person by refusing to do the right thing.

In follow-up interviews, fully 70 percent of people who were fired knew that it was coming. Their only question was why the manager took so much time to let them go. It is difficult for a person to fire himself. Even if he is in the wrong job, and dislikes the job, and is doing it poorly, and is not getting along with anyone else, he needs the manager to have the courage to put him out of his misery.

Fire Professionally

How do you fire the person who is wrong for the job? There is a simple process that is guaranteed to work and will keep you out of court, in most cases.

First, you make the decision to let the person go at a specific time on a specific day, and then you refuse to budge. You say to yourself, "I am going to call this person in at ten o'clock on Friday morning and let him or her go."

Second, when you call the person in, you close the door and sit down. (It's even better to go to the other person's office so that you can get up and leave afterward.) You then use these carefully chosen words: "I have given this situation a lot of thought. I have come to the conclusion that this is not the right job for you, and that you are not the right person for this job. And that I think that you would be happier doing something else."

Once you have begun the firing process, you absolutely refuse to discuss the past performance of the employee or anything that the individual has or has not done on the job. It is too late for that. It is all over. The job is finished. The person is gone.

Practice Broken Record

At this point, it is quite common for the employee to argue with you. The person will often be surprised, shocked, sad, crying, angry, abusive, and a variety of other things. Remember, this is a high-stress experience for the employee.

But whatever the employee says, you remain completely calm, like a stone Buddha. You nod patiently and respectfully and wait until the individual stops talking and takes a breath. Then, you repeat your previous statement: "The fact is that this is not the right job for you, and you are not the right person for this job, and I think that you will be happier doing something else."

In assertiveness training, this is called the "broken record." You repeat the same message, in the same words, in a calm tone of voice, over and over again until the other person finally gives up and accepts being fired.

Have a Plan

At this point, you can then explain what is going to happen from this moment forward. If it is an unpleasant firing, you will want the person to pack up and leave the office immediately. You will want to have someone ready to sit in with the person while he packs, to watch and make sure that he does not damage anything.

Severance pay is extremely emotional. Most people have no savings. When they are fired from a job, their first thought is often panicky. They'll wonder, "How am I going to eat or pay my rent?"

Be prepared. Prepare your severance packet in advance. Unless you have a written contract, there is no legal requirement to give a severance of any kind. But the convention is one week of severance for each year of service. Anything more or less than that is completely up to your discretion and dependent on the way people behave after learning that they have been fired.

Have a Witness

One final point: If you are a man who is firing a woman, have another woman sit in on the firing meeting with you. If you are a woman who is firing a man, have a man sit in with you. If you have the slightest concern that this person may accuse you of sexual harassment, always have an opposite sex witness in the room with you when you conduct the firing interview. In this way, you can protect yourself completely against the possibility of being sued.

There are many other tips and techniques that you can use to fire effectively. It is a skill that you must learn as part of your business skill repertoire. These basics will help you to clear out the incompetent people in your workforce who may be dragging you down and holding you back.

Remember these words of wisdom: "The best time to fire a person is the first time it crosses your mind."

THIRTEEN

Hold Effective Meetings

EASILY 25 PERCENT to 50 percent of management time is spent in meetings. Meetings are an inevitable and necessary part of organizational life. They cannot be avoided, so they must be made more effective.

The three most common types of meetings that you will have are 1) information-sharing meetings; 2) problem-solving meetings; and 3) meetings to announce new products, services, or people.

Always ask why you are having this meeting in the first place. Clarity is essential. If it is possible to avoid having a meeting, then don't have a meeting at all. Meetings can be major time wasters unless they are used properly.

Meetings are expensive. A good way to determine the cost of the meeting is to multiply the hourly salaries of the people who will be in the meeting and arrive at a total cost of taking those people out of the workforce.

In many cases, a meeting will be costing the company hundreds and even thousands of dollars. If someone came to you and asked for that amount of money in cash for an expenditure of some kind, you would probably be very careful in reviewing the expenditure and approving the amount.

Treat meetings the same way.

Prepare an Agenda

If you must have a meeting, always write out an agenda. As you write out the agenda, you will find that many of the items only affect one other person, who you can quickly telephone or e-mail.

When you write out an agenda for a meeting, use the 80/20 rule. Twenty percent of the items to be discussed will account for 80 percent of the value. Make sure that the most important items are discussed first, just in case you run out of time.

To run effective meetings, always start and stop on time. Parkinson's Law says that "work expands to fill the time allotted for it." The reverse of this law is that "work contracts to fit the time allotted for it."

If you don't have a clear stop time for the meeting, the conversation will drift in circles and the meeting can go on and on, with little result. You will, however, be happily surprised to see how many items you can cover when you have a firm stopping time.

Be Punctual

If you say that you are going to start the meeting at 10 a.m., begin punctually at that hour. Make it clear to people that if they are not in the room, they are going to miss the meeting. Some executives lock the door of the meeting room at the prescribed start time so that no one else can get in.

A good rule is to assume that latecomers are not coming at all, and just begin the meeting without them. Even if the latecomer is your boss, take responsibility for the meeting and get started.

Only invite people whose presence is essential to the business of the meeting. Sometimes we make the mistake of inviting people so that they will feel included in the work team. This is no longer necessary. People are so busy that they will always appreciate it if you excuse them from attending a meeting to which they cannot make a valuable contribution.

Let Them Leave

Allow people to leave the meeting when they are no longer necessary. Sometimes, only one item on the agenda is relevant to a particular person. If this is the case, tend to that item immediately if you can, and then let the person leave and go back to work. This is a good use of everyone's time.

As you discuss and deal with each item on the agenda, come to a resolution. Make an action decision. Assign a work responsibility with a deadline. Wrap up each point before proceeding to the next.

Over the years, I have been to countless meetings where discussions have been held and decisions have been made. Two weeks later, we are back in another meeting and nothing has been done. Why not? It was because no resolution was reached and no action was planned. No one was assigned the specific, time-bounded responsibility for taking action on a particular task.

Be Action-Oriented

My favorite question is always, "What is our next action?" Once everyone in the meeting has discussed an item, you or someone else can ask, "What is our next action?" You can even write that question on the board so that everyone can see that the point cannot be passed until some resolution has been made and some action commitment has been agreed to.

At the end of the meeting, summarize the results of the meeting. Repeat who is going to do what, and by when, and how task completion will be measured, and then thank everybody for attending. The more you make your meetings brief, to the point, and effective, the more eagerly people will attend your meetings and make their most valuable contributions.

When I hold my weekly staff meetings, the agenda consists of the name of each person in attendance. We go around the table and have people report on what they are doing, the challenges they are facing, and what their plans are for the coming week. As one person reports, each of the others is invited to ask questions for clarification. By the end of the meeting, not only is there a high level of cooperation and positive spirit, but everyone knows what everyone else is doing.

Don't Dominate

It is quite common for the meeting leader or senior executive to dominate the discussion. A good way to prevent that from happening is to assign the chairmanship of the meeting to one of your staff members, alternating this function each week. You will be amazed at how intelligent and well prepared others will be when you tell them that they are going to be in charge of the meeting.

Then, instead of dominating the conversation, you simply participate like everyone else. You will be amazed at the difference. Remember, your ability to run effective meetings is a critical executive skill. Meetings can consume an enormous amount of management time, so you owe it to yourself and your company to become absolutely excellent at extracting the highest value from every minute spent in a meeting.

FOURTEEN

Build Team Spirit

TEAM BUILDING is an essential skill of effective managers. The ability to assemble and work with an effective team is a key requirement for promotion and also one of the top qualities that companies look for when seeking out high-potential managers. Your ability to create a peak performing team is absolutely essential to your success.

Stanford Graduate School of Business did a thirty-year research project into the qualities necessary to become a senior executive of a large corporation. The researchers found that the CEOs of Fortune 500 companies all seemed to have two major qualities in common.

The first was the ability to function well in a crisis. "When the going gets tough, the tough get going." This talent, demonstrated early in their careers, allowed them to bounce back from problems and setbacks, deal with them effectively, and push through to achieve company goals.

Be a Team Player

The second quality that top executives had in common was the capacity to form and work as part of a team. When they started their careers, they were excellent team players. They volunteered for every assignment. They quickly moved into the top 20 percent of team members who do 80 percent of the work.

As a result, they were promoted and given people to supervise, who became part of their team. As they accomplished more results by working effectively with their team members, they were given more and more team members to work with. Later on in their careers, as CEOs of Fortune 500 corporations, they found themselves with tens of thousands of people working under them in different capacities.

But here's what they also found in this study: The ability to function well in a crisis could not be taught in a classroom. It had to come from within the individual. But the ability to be an excellent team player, and to build teams that accomplished great results for the company, was a learnable skill.

A Learnable Skill

You become an excellent team leader and build team spirit by doing several things in sequence.

First, be very clear about who you are and what you want. Determine your strengths and your weaknesses. Set clear goals and objectives for yourself and your career, and then clear goals and objectives for your area of responsibility.

Second, take the time to tell people what they, collectively, as a team, are doing and why. Especially, define the team's goals and mission in terms of how the work helps and improves the lives of other people. Make it an inspiring concept so that people will want to be a member of the team that is bringing about this result.

I met the president of Walmart just after he gave a speech at the company's annual convention in Saint Louis, attended by 25,000 Walmart managers and employees. He knew what his values, vision, mission, and purpose truly were. Here is what he said: "We here at Walmart know exactly what we are doing. Our goal is to provide the very best selection of products and services at the lowest possible price to our customers so that they have more money to spend on their families and children."

The entire room rose and gave him a standing ovation. Their passion for helping to improve the lives of their customers and their families is the driving force of the entire organization.

Talk and Share Ideas

There is a direct relationship between regular communications and team spirit. Hold effective meetings with your staff every week to share ideas and find out what everyone is doing.

Every successful company I have worked with continually seeks out reasons to bring its people together in ways that build spirit, motivation, and dedication to the organization. Wells Fargo bank, for example, is famous for encouraging each branch office to select a charity that everyone in the branch contributes to and supports, even in a small way. This idea has been so successful at building high levels of team spirit in each branch that Wells Fargo now dedicates more than 100 full-time people at headquarters to support this initiative.

Celebrate Important Events

Celebrate birthdays, successes, and victories with prizes and recognition. Make people feel important. When people are praised and celebrated, they feel terrific about themselves and their other team members.

Encourage a climate of harmony. My friend Ken Blanchard, with 172 people in his organization, calls himself the "chief spiritual officer." He says that his job is to ensure that there is a high level of harmony and happiness among all the staff members. This is one of the most important things you can do as a team leader.

In our company, we tell employees that we want them to be happy in their jobs. I say, "If you have any problems or concerns, please come to me or one of the other executives and we will try to resolve the problem for you." But if we find a person who is negative or unhappy for any period of time, and who cannot be satisfied, we encourage that person to go and work somewhere else. One unhappy or negative person in a work environment can poison the attitudes of many people.

Keep People Informed

Keep people informed about everything that is going on in the company that affects their work. Tell them how the changing economy might affect their sales and their jobs. Tell them how changes in staff and personnel will affect their jobs and their activities. The more people know about what is going on in their work environment, the more positive and dedicated they are when functioning as members of a team.

Three Levels of Development

There are three levels of development that people go through in their work life. The first is *dependence*, where they rely on other people to tell them what to do and to provide their workplace, paycheck, and benefits.

The second and higher level is *independence*. Here, the individual feels competent in his ability to do his work and be recognized for it.

The third level of development is *interdependence*. It is the highest level of all. At this level, each person works in cooperation with others to accomplish a job that would be impossible for one person to accomplish working on his own.

A way to encourage independence, which is a positive quality, is to establish rewards for independent achievements (namely, for individual accomplishments).

The way that you encourage interdependence is by establishing group rewards, or rewards that are divided up among the individuals on the team on some basis. Rewards can be profit sharing, bonuses, and even celebrations, such as parties, vacations, and company outings, as examples. The more that you bring your team members together to discuss and work together in a spirit of harmony, the more positive and motivated they will feel, and the more committed they will be to your company and to the accomplishment of your goals.

FIFTEEN

Make Good Decisions

DECISIVENESS IS a key quality of effective managers. No promotion or advancement is possible until a person develops the ability to solve problems and make good decisions.

On occasion, I tell the managers in my audiences that I have a remarkable memory. I have learned how to memorize the job title of every single person in the room. Because there may be several hundred people present, everyone looks at me with some skepticism while I go on to explain what I mean. "No matter what title or position is written on your business card," I say, "your true job description is problem solver."

From the time you start work in the morning until the time you go home at night, you are solving problems, big and small, one after the other, nonstop. If there weren't any problems for you to solve, your job could be replaced by a machine or by a junior employee.

Become Solution-Oriented

Average people think continually about the problems they are facing and who is to blame for those problems. Top people think continually about the solutions to the problems they have and what actions can be taken immediately to move ahead. The key is to grow your ability as a problem solver.

Whenever you experience frustration, resistance, or a setback of any kind, begin by asking, "What exactly is the problem?"

Define the problem in as many different ways as possible. You can even contemplate this question: "Is this really a problem? Could this situation be a benefit or an advantage? Could it be a blessing in disguise?" Sometimes, the problem you are dealing with is not the real problem at all.

Beware of a problem for which there is only one definition. The more ways that you can define a problem, the more amenable it becomes to a solution and to a decision that will really get results.

Once you have defined the problem, you then ask, "What are all the possible solutions?" Beware of a problem for which there is only one solution. The more solutions that you consider, the more likely it is that you will come up with the ideal solution that will bring about the best result.

Make a Decision

Finally, make a decision. Decide exactly what you are going to do to resolve the problem, overcome the obstacle, or achieve the goal.

Having made your decision, assign specific responsibility for that decision to someone on your staff or else to yourself. Set a deadline. A decision without a deadline is merely a conversation without a resolution.

In an earlier chapter, I talked about Daniel Kahneman's observations of the difference between fast thinking and slow thinking. Fully 80 percent of decisions at work can be taken care of with fast thinking. You probably have most of the facts and information you require. Decision making requires a choice between one course of action or another. You choose one course of action and get busy. Usually any action is better than no action at all.

Use Slow Thinking

Only 20 percent of decisions require slow thinking. In cases where the potential consequences of a wrong decision can be significant, you need to slow down, gather more information, and take your time.

The rule is that if it is not necessary to decide, it is necessary not to decide—at least for the time being. Recent research shows that the more time you put between the information-gathering stage and the decision stage, the better your decision will be overall. Always delay making an important decision, of any kind, for as long as you can. Your decision, in the end, will always be superior to one that is made without enough slow thinking.

Once you make a decision, assign responsibility, set a deadline, and follow up. You are on your way. This is your job. This is why you are on the payroll, to make decisions.

Cut Your Losses

One final point with regard to problem solving and decision making: In each case, you make the best decisions that you can with what you know at that moment. If you receive new information that changes the situation, be prepared to cut your losses and make a new decision.

There is a Turkish proverb that says, "No matter how long you have gone down the wrong road, turn back."

When you practice these principles, you will become a better problem solver and decision maker. And as Henry Kissinger said, "The only reward that you get for solving problems is even bigger problems to solve."

The most successful people, those who are paid the most and promoted the fastest to the highest positions in the organization, are those who have developed a proven ability to solve each problem that they meet at their level, using them as stepping-stones to even greater things. And you can do the same.

SIXTEEN

Remove Obstacles
to Performance

BETWEEN YOU and anything you want to accomplish in
your business or personal life, there will always be obstacles to overcome and roadblocks that you will have to go
over or around. Your ability to deal with the inevitable
obstacles to success in life is a learnable skill. This ability
can do more to help you achieve your goals than perhaps
any other skill.

In goal-setting programs, I always ask the question, "Once
you have determined your goal, what are all the obstacles
that stand between you and your goal at this time?"

Another way to phrase this question is, "Why aren't you
already at your goal? What is holding you back?"

People often mistake a goal for an activity. They say, "I
have a goal list for each day." But it's not a goal list; it's a

"to-do list." A goal is something bigger, something that requires overcoming difficulties and solving problems. A goal is something that requires courage, persistence, and determination to achieve. It is not simply an activity or something "to do."

Determine Your Goals

Begin by determining your most important goals in your work. Why are you on the payroll? What goals have you been hired to achieve? Of all the goals that you can achieve, which are the most important in determining your value and your contribution?

You then ask, "Why aren't I already at this goal? What is holding me back?"

The Principle of Constraints

Eliyahu Goldratt, a management consultant, first wrote about the principle of constraints in his book *The Goal*, and it is perhaps one of the biggest breakthroughs in management. His idea is simple and can be revolutionary for you.

Goldratt said that between wherever you are and wherever you want to go, there is a path that you need to follow. But along this track there is a choke point or constraint that determines how fast you achieve that goal.

The key question is, "What one factor determines the speed at which I achieve this particular goal?"

When we work with sales organizations, we find that the number one goal of almost every company is high sales. We then define the problem or constraint by saying, "Our sales are not high enough."

But what else is the problem? We have found that there are as many as twenty-one different reasons why a company's sales are not high enough. And in most cases, the companies are working busily to solve the wrong problem. They are not dealing with the real constraint or bottleneck at all.

The 80/20 Rule Revisited

With regard to constraints, or the factors that are holding you back from achieving your goals, we have found that the 80/20 rule applies. In this case, we find that 80 percent of the reasons why you are not successful in achieving a particular goal are within yourself or within your business. Only 20 percent of the constraints are on the outside, contained in the market, the competition, or other factors.

The starting point, then, of identifying and alleviating your constraints is to ask the question, "What is it *in me* that is holding me back?"

When you begin by looking into yourself or your business for the reasons, you will often find out exactly why you are not achieving the goals that you have set for yourself.

Identify Individual Constraints

As a manager, one of your most important jobs is to help your employees to identify the key constraint that is holding them back from achieving their most important results. Whether the constraint is a lack of instruction, resources, facilities, money, time, or something else, whenever possible, it is your job as a manager to help employees remove that obstacle or constraint so that they can perform at their best.

Once you have defined the key constraint, focus all your time and attention on alleviating that constraint or limiting factor to success. Concentrate single-mindedly on that one element, that one constraint, to the exclusion of every other activity. Once you alleviate or remove your biggest constraint or obstacle, you'll start to make more progress, faster, than from any other activity you engage in.

SEVENTEEN

Become a Role Model

ONE OF THE most important contributions you can make to your business is to become a role model to your staff. You should strive to become the kind of person that people look up to, admire, and want to be like.

Excellent managers know that they are constantly being observed by their staff and that their behavior sets the standard for the entire work unit. Remember that your people will work the way you do. If you want people to come in early in the morning, you come in early. If you want them to be punctual, make a habit of being punctual yourself. If you want them to set priorities on their tasks, you should set priorities on your tasks. If you want them to use their time well, you should use your time well.

Set the Standard

Your organization or department will eventually take on the attitudes, values, opinions, behaviors, and habits that you demonstrate. Ralph Waldo Emerson said, "Every organization is merely the lengthened shadow of one man." You can never expect people in your organization to be much different or much better than you are.

One of the great questions to ask is, "What kind of a company would it be if everyone in it was just like me?"

When you ask and answer this question, over and over, you will always see areas where you could improve and become both a better manager and a better person.

It is up to you to set higher standards for yourself, and then to continue to raise the bar.

The Loneliness of Command

When you are a member of the staff, you can "let it all hang out." You can chitchat with coworkers, grumble about the company or other people, take long lunches, and come in to work late and leave early.

But when you become a manager, a leader, everything changes. You are no longer one of the gang. Your primary loyalty is no longer to your coworkers but to your superiors. You are expected to set the standards for everyone who reports to you.

Here's an exercise for you: Make a list of the work habits and behaviors of the ideal employee. If all your employees were perfect, how would they work, walk, talk, and interact with each other?

Then, make a list of all of those behaviors that you could *personally* engage in, in order to set an example for the behaviors that you most want to see in others. Review these behaviors on a regular basis and look for every opportunity to practice these behaviors in your interactions with other people.

Walk the Talk

For example, if you want your employees to treat each other with caring, courtesy, and consideration, then you should make a point of practicing those same three qualities in every interaction with every staff member. Act as though everyone is watching, because everyone is watching.

Never say anything about a staff member that you do not want to have reported back to that staff member (and to everyone else in your department) within a few minutes. There are no secrets in a work environment. Everyone knows everything, and far faster than you would like.

If you want people to have good work habits, establish good work habits for yourself. If you want people to be fully prepared for meetings, come to each meeting fully prepared. Imagine that you are a teacher and that, in their day-to-day work, all your "students" are eventually going to do exactly what you do.

Becoming a role model that everyone admires and looks up to is one of the most important contributions that you can make to your business. It is for you to set high standards to which everyone wants to aspire.

EIGHTEEN

Brainstorm for Solutions

CREATIVITY AND innovation are absolutely essential to the survival of any organization in any business today. One of your responsibilities is to encourage each employee to function at the highest level of creativity possible for that person. One idea from one person who has been encouraged to think creatively can often make or save the company thousands of dollars and even hundreds of hours of work. But you never know what that one idea is likely to be, so you have to encourage a large number of ideas. There seems to be a direct relationship between the quantity of ideas generated and the quality of those ideas.

Perhaps the most powerful way to stimulate the creativity of the members of your team is to regularly practice brainstorming. The concept of brainstorming was developed by advertising executive Alex Osborn in 1946. It has since swept the world and is used by the most successful individuals and organizations in every field.

Here is how it works: First, decide to bring your people together once a week, or more frequently, to brainstorm on the problems facing the company, such as increasing sales, cutting costs, boosting revenues, reducing expenditures, and improving productivity. There are no limits to the problems that you can put on the table during a brainstorming session.

Second, create a brainstorming group. The ideal group size is four to seven people. If you have fewer than four people you will not get enough ideas. If you have more than seven in the group, many people will not have an opportunity to contribute fully.

Third, set a time limit. The ideal length for a brainstorming session is fifteen to forty-five minutes. It is a good idea to use a stopwatch or a clock and to start the brainstorming session as you would a race; then cut the session off sharp at the agreed minute. This knowledge of a fixed stop-and-start time triggers higher levels of creativity and a greater outpouring of ideas.

Fourth, define the problem or goal clearly. Write it on a whiteboard, flipchart, or a piece of paper so that everyone can see it, read it, and be completely clear about the question or problem that you are working on. If necessary, have a discussion beforehand where you agree that there is a problem to solve and also agree on a definition of that problem or obstacle before you begin generating ideas or solutions.

Fifth, pose a specific question demanding concrete answers. For example: How can we increase our sales by more than 20 percent over the next ninety days? How can we cut our costs in this area by 20 percent over the next ninety days? The best questions demand practical ideas. They force each person to think in concrete terms and generate workable solutions that can be implemented immediately.

Sixth, agree that everyone will suspend judgment during the session. No one will give either positive or negative comments and there will be no discussion or evaluation of ideas until after the brainstorming session. By agreeing to suspend judgment, you encourage ridiculous answers, laughter, and unorthodox approaches to solving the problem.

A Brainstorming Breakthrough

In the early days of space exploration and the moon program in the 1950s and 1960s, the dilemma faced by NASA scientists was weight. How could they send a rocket ship to the moon, get it to land and then take off from the moon, and fly back to earth? The problem was that if the rocket had enough fuel to break loose of the earth's gravity and land on the moon, it would not have enough fuel to then break loose of the moon's gravity and return to earth.

As a result of brainstorming, they came up with an idea that transformed the next fifty years of space travel. They said, "Why would we have to land the entire rocket on the moon? What if we just dropped a 'moon module' from the bigger spaceship that would continue in orbit around the moon, and then the smaller moon module could blast off and rejoin the larger ship for the return to earth?"

In retrospect, this sounds like a simple idea, but it was one of the greatest scientific breakthroughs in modern history. And it was a result of generating idea after idea and "thinking outside the box" to find different ways to solve a major dilemma.

Get Organized

In each brainstorming session, you need both a leader and a recorder. The leader is the person who encourages everyone to contribute ideas. The leader keeps the brainstorming session going by moving from person to person. No one is allowed to dominate the conversation.

The recorder is the person who writes down the ideas that are generated. Once the brainstorming session is complete, the ideas written down by the recorder are then turned over to the manager for evaluation at a later time.

When you conduct brainstorming sessions on company time, you show people that their thinking and creative capacity are both needed and respected in the company. When you ask people to think creatively, they will astonish you with the ideas that they come up with. You will be amazed at how creative the average person is if given a chance and asked to contribute.

After the brainstorming session, people will come up to you continually with new ideas that just popped into their heads while they were working. When you make it a habit of stimulating the creativity of your staff members, they will begin to think creatively all day long. And sometimes one good idea can change the entire future of your business.

NINETEEN

Negotiate Like a Professional

ALL GOOD managers are excellent negotiators. The manager is usually involved in a continuous process of negotiating conflicting interests and views. All work life is "different strokes for different folks."

When you are negotiating on your own, or on behalf of your company, there is a process that you can follow to ensure that you get the best deal for yourself and your business.

Follow a Process

First, before you go into a negotiation, take some time to think about what the ideal solution would be for you if this negotiation worked out perfectly.

A person who has thought about the factors or decisions involved, has developed alternatives, and has a clear idea of what, ideally, should be accomplished has a tremendous advantage over another person who walks into a negotiation without having given it much thought. At least 80 percent of negotiating success is preparation.

There is no such thing as "too much preparation" when you are entering into an important negotiation that involves a lot of money or has large potential consequences for your company. Take the time to think on paper and write out exactly what you want, point for point, before you meet with the other party.

Prepare the Other Side First

Once you are clear about your ideal desired outcome, use the "lawyer's method of preparation." Make a list of everything that you think that the other party will want to achieve in this negotiation. Just as lawyers are trained to prepare the case of their opposition before they prepare their own case, you do the same in preparation for the negotiation. Put yourself in their shoes and think through their positions or demands in advance.

Be Easy to Work With

Resolve to be an excellent negotiating partner. The best negotiators are warm, friendly, calm, courteous, and helpful. They treat their negotiation counterparts with respect and politeness. They strive to make the other parties comfortable by getting them a cup of coffee or a glass of water and by positioning themselves as friends in the negotiation.

One of the most powerful factors to ensure that you get the best deal possible in a negotiation is "likability." The more that the other person likes you, the more open that person is to being influenced by you, even to the point of making concessions to make you happy with the result of the negotiation.

Forget everything you have read or heard about hardball negotiating. It only works in the movies. If you try to be difficult or demanding in a negotiation, there is a very high likelihood that the other party will simply terminate the discussion or walk out. If someone is being difficult with you in a negotiation, resolve to be relaxed and cheerful and wait for the person to settle down.

Strive for a Win-Win Solution

The ideal negotiating result is called a win-win. It's where both parties feel that they have gotten a good deal in the negotiation. Both parties feel that they have won in some way. Neither party leaves dissatisfied or unhappy with the result of the negotiation.

Remember, the purpose of a business negotiation is to enter into an agreement so that both parties are sufficiently happy with the result that they both carry out their commitments under the negotiation and are open to negotiating with the same party again in the future.

Think Long Term

Personally, I have business relationships that have involved negotiations that go back more than twenty-five years.

Because I have always been prepared and fair—seeking a win-win result—over the years I have been able to enter into many millions of dollars' worth of negotiations with the same parties, and I continue to do business with these parties without tension or stress. This should be your aim as well.

When you begin a negotiation, the first thing you must do is find out exactly what the other person wants and in what order of importance. You then tell the other person what you want in your order of importance.

The Law of Four

Remember the Law of Four in negotiating. This law states that, in any negotiation, there are usually only four main issues to be resolved. There is one major issue and three minor issues. The reason that a negotiation can proceed is that the major issue for each of the parties is different. Each party places a greater emphasis on one of the terms or conditions and a minor emphasis on three others, and they are different from each party.

Be Prepared to Renegotiate

Negotiating terms and conditions with long-term potential consequences is another area that requires "slow thinking" if you want to get the best deal. Remember, too, that no negotiation is ever final. If based on new information or changing circumstances you find that you have made a bad deal (or, likewise, if the other party finds that it has made a bad deal), be prepared to reopen the negotiation and adjust the terms and conditions so that both parties remain happy with the agreement. When both parties are happy with the agreement, and remain happy, they will both work together to make the negotiation successful and to enter into subsequent successful negotiations in the future.

TWENTY

Communicate with Clarity

EIGHTY-FIVE percent of managerial success is contained in the manager's ability to communicate effectively with others. Almost all problems in all relationships, including business and personal relationships, are communications problems.

You have probably had the experience of listening to a person talk at length about a product, service, problem, or a course of action and afterward you still had no idea what he was talking about. This is why clarity is so important in communication. You must be perfectly clear about what it is you want to say, and then be clear in the way that you say it or communicate it to another person.

The Process of Communicating

In a communication, there is a process that takes place. To begin, you think a thought that you then translate into words and say to the other person. The other person hears the words, translates your meaning, and then replies. Words are sounds that go through the air, like radio waves, and hit your brain, where you absorb them, translate their meaning, and then reply in turn.

In this communication process, there are many opportunities for misunderstanding. You could use a word that triggers a different reaction from what you had expected. You could use a word that means something different to the person who is listening. You could mispronounce a word so that it is "garbled in translation."

When the other person hears your message, she may translate it differently from what you said. What the other person says in response to your words may mean something different from what you hear. There could be noise or distraction in the room, someone walking in or out, or a car passing by, all of which can break the flow of communications and distract either the speaker or the listener.

Preoccupation Distorts Communication

A communications breakdown can be caused by the individual thinking about a fight he had with his wife that morning, a speeding ticket he got on the way to work, something his boss said a few minutes ago, and an upcoming meeting for which he is not prepared. All of these different forms of "noise" can lead to misunderstandings.

If the first watchword in communications is *clarity*, then the second must be *patience*. Take your time to communicate slowly and then double-check to be sure that what you said was what the other person heard, and that what the other person said was what you heard and understood as well.

Three Tools of Communication

Managers have three tools of communication: the written word, the one-on-one communication, and the presentation before several people.

You must become excellent in each of these areas of communication.

First, learn how to write well. There are many excellent courses on business writing that can turn any intelligent person into an excellent writer in just a one- or two-day workshop. Written communication requires clarity, brevity, simplicity, and accuracy. Your writing skills can be improved through learning and practice. Your ability to write an excellent letter or proposal can accelerate your career and increase your influence immeasurably.

Second, learn how to communicate one-on-one. Just as in negotiating, preparation is the key to success in individual communication. Prepare your message thoroughly in advance, always thinking about the answer to the question, "What's in it for the other person?"

People do things for their reasons, not yours. If you want to influence other people and persuade them to your way of thinking, you have to offer something that they want, need, and are willing to sacrifice for.

All top managers are good at selling ideas. Always present your ideas in terms of benefits—that is, in terms of improvements in the life and work of the other person and in achieving results better, faster, and easier.

Learn to Speak on Your Feet

Third, learn how to stand up in front of an audience and give an effective presentation. The ability to "speak on your feet" is one of the most important skills you will develop as an executive, even if you start off absolutely terrified of public speaking.

You can join Toastmasters International and attend weekly meetings. You can take a Dale Carnegie course where, over fourteen weeks, you will learn to become both competent and confident on your feet. You can take a course or a seminar on professional speaking.

When you learn how to speak well and give good presentations at meetings, both within the company and outside the company, you will be astonished at how much this talent will help you in your career.

Present New Ideas Slowly

Whenever you introduce a new idea to others, you should expect resistance. Instead of rushing and insisting that people immediately do something different, you will be more persuasive if you go slowly.

Present your new idea by saying something like, "I have been thinking that there is a way that we can improve the way we are doing things. I've come up with some ways to save money or cut costs. What do you think of this idea?"

Whenever you present an idea tentatively—as though it had just occurred to you and, as such, you are interested in the opinions or ideas of others—you'll notice that people's resistance drops and their openness to being influenced by you increases.

The Seventy-Two-Hour Rule

Many years ago, I read a little book called *Time Out for Mental Digestion*. This book explained that it takes people about seventy-two hours to get their mind around a new idea. If you present a new idea and then demand an immediate response, people will almost always resist or say no. But if you present an idea and give people three days or more to think about it, they will often come back to you with even more ideas on how to make your initial idea successful.

The key to effective communications is for you to make a decision to become absolutely excellent at getting your message across in the three ways that we talked about: through written communication, individual (one-on-one) communication, and presentations in front of an audience. All communications skills are learnable. No matter where you are starting, you can become excellent at communicating effectively and influencing others to cooperate with you.

TWENTY-ONE

Achieve Personal Excellence

THERE IS probably nothing that will affect your career more for the rest of your life than your making a commitment to becoming personally excellent at the most important things that you do.

In every organization, there are two routes to the top. One route is through performance. The other route is through politics. Studies done on Machiavelli and management show that if you try to get to the top through politics, you will almost invariably be derailed some time in your career.

Dan Kennedy says, "Be careful who you step on when you are climbing the ladder of success because they will be waiting for you with drawn daggers on the way down."

Focus on Performance

When you decide to get to the top based on excellent performance, almost everyone in the organization will help you, including the people above you—your superiors—the people at your level, and your subordinates. Commit today to becoming the very best manager that you can possibly be.

It turns out that anything else less than a commitment to excellence becomes an unconscious acceptance of mediocrity. As Pat Riley, the basketball coach, has said, "If you are not getting better, you are getting worse."

Average performance is the "default setting" for virtually everyone. To override this automatic setting, you must instead make a commitment to become one of the very best people at what you do. In addition, you must set standards of excellence for everyone else who works for you. Encourage, reward, and compliment quality work. You will always be judged on the basis of the quality of the work of the people who have been entrusted to your supervision.

Celebrate Success

To encourage even higher quality, celebrate success and achievement. Give rewards and prizes. Catch people doing something right. Praise people whenever they do something that is out of the ordinary. As the song says, "Little things mean a lot."

Most important, lead by example. Look upon yourself as the standard-bearer of your department, unit, or company. When you see yourself as a role model, an example for others to follow, you put yourself on the high road to leadership in your organization and in your life.

Dedicate yourself to CANEI—continuous and never-ending improvement. Read and learn in your field each day. Attend additional courses and seminars. Listen to audio programs in your car and on your smartphone. Never stop learning and growing until you become the best manager in your business.

Conclusion

SUCCESSFUL MANAGERS are made, not born. They are self-made, through continuous and never-ending work on themselves. Everyone starts at the bottom and then works his or her way up through hard, hard work, sustained over a long period of time.

You can become an excellent manager when you learn and practice the behaviors, methods, and techniques of other successful managers. If you do what other successful people do, you will soon get the results that other successful people get.

The ideas and strategies contained in this book are based on more than thirty years of research and experience in large and small companies. If you recognize that you have room to improve in any one of these twenty-one areas, resolve right now—today—to do something about it. Read a book, take a seminar, listen to an audio program, or ask for advice from people you look up to and admire. Dedicate yourself to continuous self-improvement as if your entire future depended on it. Because it does.

ABOUT THE AUTHOR

Brian Tracy is a professional speaker, trainer, seminar leader, and consultant, and chairman of Brian Tracy International, a training and consulting company based in Solana Beach, California.

Brian bootstrapped his way to success. In 1981, in talks and seminars around the U.S., he began teaching the principles he forged in sales and business. Today, his books and audio and video programs—more than 500 of them—are available in 38 languages and are used in 55 countries.

He is the bestselling author of more than fifty books, including *Full Engagement* and *Reinvention*.

"Inspiring, entertaining, informative, motivational..."
Brian Tracy is one of the world's top speakers. He addresses more than 250,000 people annually—in over 100 appearances—and has consulted and trained at more than 1,000 corporations. In his career he has reached over five million people in 58 countries. He has lived and practiced every principle in his writing and speeches:

21st-Century Thinking: How to outmaneuver the competition and get superior results in an ever-turbulent business climate.

Leadership in the New Millennium: Learn the most powerful leadership principles—ever—to get maximum results, faster.

Advanced Selling Strategies: How to use modern sales' most advanced strategies and tactics to outperform your competitors.

The Psychology of Success: Think and act like the top performers. Learn practical, proven techniques for excellence.

To book Brian to speak at your next meeting or conference, visit Brian Tracy International at www.briantracy.com, or call (858) 436-7316 for a free promotional package. Brian will carefully customize his talk to your specific needs.